JONES & BARTLETT LEARNING INFORMATION SYSTEMS SECURITY & ASSURANCE SERIES

LABORATORY MANUAL TO ACCOMPANY

Legal Issues in Information Security

1E REVISED

VLAB SOLUTIONS

JONES & BARTLETT LEARNING

World Headquarters
Jones & Bartlett Learning
5 Wall Street
Burlington, MA 01803
978-443-5000
info@jblearning.com
www.jblearning.com

Jones & Bartlett Learning books and products are available through most bookstores and online booksellers. To contact Jones & Bartlett Learning directly, call 800-832-0034, fax 978-443-8000, or visit our website, www.jblearning.com.

Substantial discounts on bulk quantities of Jones & Bartlett Learning publications are available to corporations, professional associations, and other qualified organizations. For details and specific discount information, contact the special sales department at Jones & Bartlett Learning via the above contact information or send an email to specialsales@jblearning.com.

Production Credits
Chief Executive Officer: Ty Field
President: James Homer
SVP, Editor-in-Chief: Michael Johnson
SVP, Chief Marketing Officer: Alison M. Pendergast
SVP, Curriculum Solutions: Christopher Will
Director of Sales, Curriculum Solutions: Randi Roger
Author: vLab Solutions, LLC, David Kim, President
Editorial Management: High Stakes Writing, LLC, Lawrence J. Goodrich, Editor and Publisher
Copy Editor, High Stakes Writing: Katherine Dillin
Senior Editorial Assistant: Rainna Erikson
Reprints and Special Projects Manager: Susan Schultz
Production Editor: Tina Chen
Rights & Photo Research Associate: Lian Bruno
Manufacturing and Inventory Control Supervisor: Amy Bacus
Senior Marketing Manager: Andrea DeFronzo
Cover Design: Anne Spencer
Composition: CAE Solutions Corp.
Cover Image: © Julien Tromeur/ShutterStock, Inc.
Printing and Binding: Edwards Brothers Malloy
Cover Printing: Edwards Brothers Malloy

ISBN: 978-1-4496-3846-7

6048
Printed in the United States of America
16 15 14 13 12   10 9 8 7 6 5 4 3 2

Contents

Ethics and Code of Conduct

The material presented in this course is designed to give you a real-life look at the use of various tools and systems that are at the heart of every network security analyst's daily responsibilities. Through use of this material, you will have access to software and techniques used every day by professionals. With this access come certain ethical responsibilities.

The hardware, software, tools, and applications presented and used in this lab manual and/or the VSCL are intended to be used for instructional and educational purposes only.

As a student in this course, you are not to use these tools, applications, or techniques on live production IT infrastructures inside or outside of your campus or organization. Under no circumstances are you permitted to use these tools, applications, or techniques on the production IT infrastructures and networks of other organizations.

You are required to conform to your school or organization's Code of Conduct and ethics policies during the use of this lab manual and any of the tools, applications, or techniques described within.

Preface

Welcome! This lab manual is your step-by-step guide to completing the laboratory exercises for this course.

How to Use This Lab Manual

This lab manual features step-by-step instructions for completing the following hands-on lab exercises:

VSCL	LAB TITLE
No	Lab #1: Create an IT Infrastructure Asset List and Identify Where Privacy Data Resides
No	Lab #2: Case Study on U.S. Veterans Affairs and Loss of Privacy Information
No	Lab #3: Case Study on PCI DSS Non-Compliance: CardSystems Solutions
No	Lab #4: Analyze and Compare GLBA and HIPAA
No	Lab #5: Case Study on Issues Related to Sharing Consumers' Confidential Information
No	Lab #6: Identify the Scope of Your State's Data and Security Breach Notification Law
No	Lab #7: Case Study on Digital Millennium Copyright Act: Napster
No	Lab #8: Cyberstalking or Cyberbullying and Laws to Protect Individuals
No	Lab #9: Recommend IT Security Policies to Help Mitigate Risk
No	Lab #10: Case Study in Computer Forensics: Pharmaceutical Company

Paper-Based Labs

The labs in this manual are paper-based and do not require use of the Virtual Security Cloud Lab (VSCL). To successfully complete the deliverables for this lab, you will need access to a text editor or word processor, such as Microsoft® Word. For some labs, you may also need access to a PDF reader and a graphics line drawing application, such as Visio or PowerPoint.

Note:

If you don't have a word processor or graphics package, use OpenOffice on the student landing Workstation for your lab deliverables and to answer the lab assessment questions. To capture screenshots, **press Prt Sc > MSPAINT, paste** into a text document, and **save** the document in the Security_Strategies folder **(C:\Security_Strategies\)** using the File Transfer function.

Step-by-Step Instructions

You'll find it easy to complete these lab exercises by following the detailed step-by-step instructions. Each step is clearly broken down into sub-steps, and all actions you are required to take are noted in **bold** font. If you get stuck on a step, please consult your syllabus or instructor.

Some of these lab exercises require the use of the Internet. The VSCL environment does not include live Internet access. To successfully complete these steps, you will need to use a workstation with Internet access.

Deliverables

At the completion of each lab, you'll be asked to provide a set of deliverables to your instructor. These deliverables may include documents, files, screenshots, and/or answers to assessment questions. The deliverables are designed to test your understanding of the information, and your successful completion of the steps and functions of the lab. For specific information on deliverables, refer to the **Deliverables** section at the end of each lab.

Note:

Use of this lab manual or the VSCL **does not require use of the textbook**. If you have questions about whether a textbook is needed for your course, consult your instructor.

Create an IT Infrastructure Asset List and Identify Where Privacy Data Resides

LAB 1

Introduction

The purpose of an IT asset identification and asset classification exercise is to protect privacy data and implement security controls. Identifying where privacy data is accessed throughout an IT infrastructure or outside of its protected environment is important. In this lab, you will create an IT asset/inventory checklist organized within the seven domains of a typical IT infrastructure, perform an asset identification and classification exercise, explain how a data classification standard is linked to customer privacy data and security controls, and identify where privacy data resides and what security controls are needed to maintain compliance.

Learning Objectives

Upon completing this lab, you will be able to:

- Create an IT asset/inventory checklist organized within the seven domains of a typical IT infrastructure
- Perform an asset identification and asset classification exercise for a typical IT infrastructure
- Explain how a data classification standard is linked to customer privacy data protection and proper security controls
- Identify where privacy data can reside or traverse throughout the seven domains of a typical IT infrastructure
- Identify where privacy data protection and proper security controls are needed to assist organizations with maintaining compliance

Deliverables

Upon completion of this lab, you are required to provide the following deliverables to your instructor:

1. IT Inventory Checklist Lab #1 text document;
2. Lab Assessment Questions & Answers for Lab #1.

Hands-On Steps

1. From your computer workstation, **create** a new text document called **IT Inventory Checklist Lab #1**.
2. **Review** the seven domains of a typical IT infrastructure.

FIGURE 1.1
Seven domains of a typical IT infrastructure

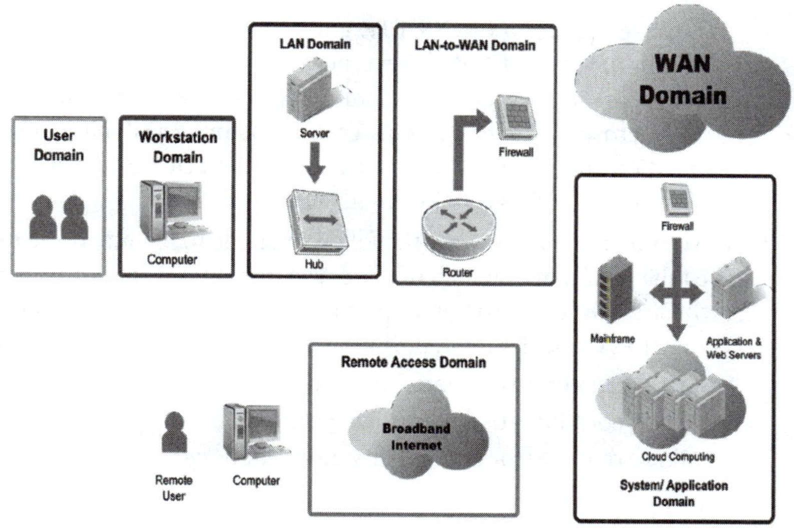

3. **Review** Figure 1.2, which is a Mock IT infrastructure with a Cisco core backbone network.

FIGURE 1.2
Mock IT infrastructure with Cisco core backbone network

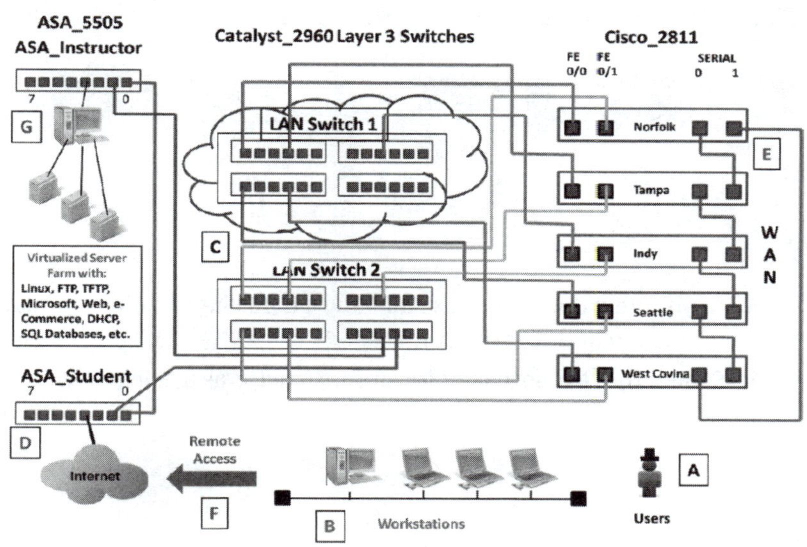

4. Refer to Figure 1.2 and **note** the following information, which describes the details of the workstation domain and systems/application domain at a health care provider under the Health Insurance Portability and Accountability Act, or HIPAA, compliance law:
   - Workstation Domain: Indicated by the "B" in Figure 1.2, the workstation domain consists of Microsoft® XP 2003, SP2 workstations (50), laptops (50), and desktop computers (50)
   - Systems/Application Domain: Indicated by the "G" in Figure 1.2, the systems/application domain consists of the following servers and applications:
     - Linux Server #1 (DNS, FTP, and TFTP)
     - Linux Server #2 (Web Server)
     - Microsoft® Server #1 (e-Commerce Server and Customer Database Subset)
     - Microsoft® Server #2 (Master SQL Customer Database and Intellectual Property Assets)
     - Microsoft® Server #3 (Office Automation, DHCP Server, and Customer Database Subset)
     - Microsoft® Server #4 (E-mail Server)
5. In your text document, use the following table to **identify** three to five IT assets and insert them into the table. **Indicate** in which of the seven domains of an IT infrastructure the asset resides. **Indicate** if the asset accesses customer privacy data or contains customer privacy data. Finally, **classify** the IT asset as Critical, Major, or Minor, where the following defines each:
   - **Critical:** generates revenues or represents intellectual property asset of organization
   - **Major:** contains customer privacy data
   - **Minor:** required for normal business functions and operations

IT ASSET DESCRIPTION	SEVEN DOMAINS OF TYPICAL IT	PRIVACY DATA IMPACT	ASSESSMENT [CRITICAL-MAJOR-MINOR]

6. In your text document, **explain** how a data classification standard is related to customer privacy data protection and security controls.
7. **Submit** the **text document** to your instructor as a deliverable for this lab.

Evaluation Criteria and Rubrics

The following are the evaluation criteria and rubrics for Lab #1 that the students must perform:

1. Was the student able to create an IT asset/inventory checklist organized within the seven domains of a typical IT infrastructure? – **[20%]**
2. Was the student able to perform an asset identification and asset classification exercise for a typical IT infrastructure? – **[20%]**
3. Was the student able to explain how a data classification standard is linked to customer privacy data protection and proper security controls? – **[20%]**
4. Was the student able to identify where privacy data may reside or traverse throughout the seven domains of a typical IT infrastructure? – **[20%]**
5. Was the student able to identify where privacy data protection and proper security controls are needed to assist organizations with maintaining compliance? – **[20%]**

LAB #1 – ASSESSMENT WORKSHEET

Create an IT Infrastructure Asset List and Identify Where Privacy Data Resides

Course Name and Number: ______________________________

Student Name: ______________________________

Instructor Name: ______________________________

Lab Due Date: ______________________________

Overview

The purpose of an IT asset identification and asset classification exercise is to protect privacy data and implement security controls. Identifying where privacy data is accessed throughout an IT infrastructure or outside of its protected environment is important. In this lab, you created an IT asset/inventory checklist organized within the seven domains of a typical IT infrastructure, performed an asset identification and classification exercise, explained how a data classification standard is linked to customer privacy data and security controls, and identified where privacy data resides and what security controls are needed to maintain compliance.

Lab Assessment Questions & Answers

1. What is the purpose of identifying IT assets and inventory?

____

____

____

____

2. What is the purpose of an asset classification?

____

____

____

____

3. Why might an organization's website classification be minor but its e-commerce server be considered critical for your scenario?

4. Why would you classify customer privacy data and intellectual property assets as critical?

5. What are some examples of security controls for recent compliance law requirements?

6. How can a data classification standard help with asset classification?

7. Given the importance of a Master SQL database that houses customer privacy data and intellectual property assets, what security controls and security countermeasures can you apply to help protect these assets?

8. From a legal and liability perspective, what recommendations do you have for ensuring the confidentiality of customer privacy data throughout the Mock IT infrastructure?

9. What can your organization document and implement to help mitigate the risks, threats, and liabilities typically found in an IT infrastructure?

10. True or false: Organizations under recent compliancy laws, such as HIPAA and the Gramm-Leach-Bliley Act (GLBA), are mandated to have documented IT security policies, standards, procedures, and guidelines.

11. Why is it important to identify where privacy data resides throughout your IT infrastructure?

LAB 2

Case Study on U.S. Veterans Affairs and Loss of Privacy Information

Introduction

The loss of privacy data has implications for both the individual(s) responsible and the organization at which the individual(s) works. Privacy and information systems security can be violated, but breaches can also be prevented. In this lab, you will review a real-world case study that involves the loss of privacy information, and you will analyze what violations occurred, the implications of those violations, and the possible mitigation remedies that can prevent future violations.

Learning Objectives

Upon completing this lab, you will be able to:

- Relate a real-world case study on privacy law violation and its implications to the individual and the organization in violation
- Distinguish how privacy law is different from information systems security
- Review a case study on a U.S. government agency's loss of privacy data and information
- Suggest possible mitigation remedies to prevent the same loss from occurring at another organization

Deliverables

Upon completion of this lab, you are required to provide the following deliverables to your instructor:

1. U.S. Veterans Affairs Case Study Lab #2 text document;
2. Lab Assessment Questions & Answers for Lab #2.

Hands-On Steps

1. From your computer workstation, **create** a new text document called **U.S. Veterans Affairs Case Study Lab #2**.
2. **Review** the following **Lab #2 Case Study on U.S. Veterans Affairs and Loss of Privacy Information**:

   The U.S. Department of Veterans Affairs had a privacy data breach in 2006 that an agency employee said affected the records of 26.5 million veterans and their spouses. An employee at the agency reported the breach and said that a laptop he used at his home in Montgomery County, Maryland, had been stolen. This employee had been taking home a laptop that contained private information of the approximately 26.5 million veterans. This privacy information included the veterans' names, Social Security numbers, the dates of birth, and disability ratings.

   On May 17, 2006, the FBI was informed of the breach, and it began an investigation along with the VA Inspector General's Office. During the investigation, it was discovered that more than the originally reported veterans and their spouses were affected by the theft. In fact, approximately 1.1 million active-duty military personnel were affected, as well as 430,000 members of the National Guard and 645,000 members of the Reserves. In addition the investigation revealed other information, including:

   - On May 3, 2006, the theft occurred. The employee whose laptop was stolen reported the theft to his supervisors at the agency and to the Maryland police.
   - On May 16, 2006, Veterans Affairs Secretary R. James Nicholson was told of the breach that resulted in unencrypted data being stolen. Supervisors at the agency knew of the theft on May 3 when it happened, but they failed to tell Mr. Nicholson until the May 16 date.
   - On May 22, 2006, the agency finally informed those who were affected by the breach. The agency announced that the laptop had been stolen. The agency reported that the information stolen included veterans' and their spouses' names, Social Security numbers, birth dates, and disability ratings. The agency said that the information did not include financial data or electronic health records.
   - The analyst who took the laptop home had been given permission to use the laptop at home. (The agency did not reveal this until after it had already said that the employee was fired for taking the laptop home.) The employee said that he had taken the laptop home regularly for three years.

   Congress held a hearing on May 25, 2006. During this hearing, Secretary Nicholson admitted that the stolen information included disability ratings for 2.6 million people.

   On June 3, the agency admitted that approximately 50,000 active-duty personnel were also affected by the stolen data. By June 6, 2006, the agency had admitted that approximately 1.1 million active-duty military personnel were affected, as well as 430,000 members of the National Guard and 645,000 members of the Reserves.

   On June 29, 2006, an unidentified person turned the laptop over to the agency, which believes it will cost $100 million to $500 million to cover the data theft losses and prevent additional losses.
3. **Launch** your Web browser. **Read** and **review** Grant Gross's online article (IDG News), "VA Ignores Cybersecurity Warnings: Government Auditors Tell House Panel That They Can't Force VA Officials to Comply with Their Recommendations," which you can find at http://www.pcworld.com/article/126093/va_ignores_cybersecurity_warnings.html.
4. In your text document, **discuss** the case study and **answer** the following questions:
   - What laws have been violated?
   - What do you think contributed to the problems that could lead to a violation of these laws?
   - What are the implications to the individual and organization of these violations?
   - What are some security controls and mitigation strategies for handling future violations? (Name three to five.)
   - How does privacy law differ from information systems security?
5. **Submit** the **text document** to your instructor as a deliverable for this lab.

Evaluation Criteria and Rubrics

The following are the evaluation criteria and rubrics for Lab #2 that the students must perform:

1. Was the student able to relate a real-world case study on privacy law violation and its implications to the individual and the organization in violation? – [**25%**]
2. Was the student able to distinguish how privacy law is different from information systems security? – [**25%**]
3. Was the student able to review a case study on a U.S. government agency's loss of privacy data and information? – [**25%**]
4. Was the student able to suggest possible mitigation remedies to prevent the same loss from occurring at another organization? – [**25%**]

LAB #2 – ASSESSMENT WORKSHEET

Case Study on U.S. Veterans Affairs and Loss of Privacy Information

Course Name and Number: ______________________________

Student Name: ______________________________

Instructor Name: ______________________________

Lab Due Date: ______________________________

Overview

The loss of privacy data has implications for both the individual(s) responsible and the organization at which the individual(s) works. Privacy and information systems security can be violated, but breaches can also be prevented. In this lab, you reviewed a real-world case study that involved the loss of privacy information, and you analyzed what violations occurred, the implications of those violations, and the possible mitigation remedies that could prevent future violations.

Lab Assessment Questions & Answers

1. What is the difference between privacy law and information systems security? How are they related?

____

____

____

____

2. Was the employee justified in taking home official data? Why or why not?

____

____

____

____

3. What are the possible consequences associated with the data loss?

4. Regarding the loss of privacy data, was there any data containing protected health information (PHI) making this a HIPAA compliance violation?

5. What action can the agency take against the concerned employee?

6. Would the response of the agency have been different had the data theft occurred at work instead of happening at the employee's residence? Why or why not?

7. Why were the VA data analyst's two supervisors reprimanded and demoted by the VA secretary? Do you think this was justified? Why or why not?

8. What was violated in this data breach?

9. If the database had been encrypted because of VA policy, would this data loss issue even have been an issue? Why or why not?

10. What risk mitigation or security control recommendations would you suggest to prevent this from occurring again?

11. What information systems security and privacy security policies do you think would help mitigate this breach and loss of privacy data?

12. What or who was the weakest link in this chain of security and protection of privacy data?

13. If the VA had performed a security and information assurance audit for compliance, what could the VA do on an annual basis to help mitigate this type of loose policy conformance?

14. True or false: U.S. taxpayers ended up paying for this VA security breach, notifications, and post-mortem damage control.

15. Which organization in the U.S. federal government is responsible for performing audits on other U.S. federal government agencies? (Hint: It is also known as the "Congressional Watchdog.")

Case Study on PCI DSS Non-Compliance: CardSystems Solutions

LAB 3

Introduction

Payment Card Industry Data Security Standard (PCI DSS) is a compliance standard that helps prevent private data breaches in companies. In this lab, you will review a real-world case study that involves a PCI DSS non-compliance scenario, and you will recommend mitigation remedies to prevent the loss of private data for similar organizations.

Learning Objectives

Upon completing this lab, you will be able to:

- Relate a real-world case study on the Payment Card Industry Data Security Standard (PCI DSS) standard non-compliance and its implications
- Distinguish how the Payment Card Industry Data Security Standard (PCI DSS) is a standard and not a law, and how it defines requirements for information systems security controls and countermeasures
- Review a case study on a credit card transaction processing company's non-compliance with the Payment Card Industry Data Security Standard (PCI DSS) and identify the privacy data breach that occurred
- Recommend PCI DSS-compliant mitigation remedies to prevent the same loss from occurring again at a similar organization

Deliverables

Upon completion of this lab, you are required to provide the following deliverables to your instructor:

1. PCI DSS Case Study Lab #3 text document;
2. Lab Assessment Questions & Answers for Lab #3.

Hands-On Steps

1. From your computer workstation, **create** a new text document called **PCI DSS Case Study Lab #3**.
2. **Review** the Payment Card Industry Data Security Standard (PCI DSS) overview in Figure 3.1. In your text document, **explain** how PCI DSS is a standard and not a law and **discuss** how it defines requirements for information systems security controls and countermeasures.

FIGURE 3.1

PCI DSS v1.2 Information Systems Security Requirements

PCI Data Security Standard—High-Level Overview

Build and Maintain a Secure Network

Requirement 1: Install and maintain a firewall configuration to protect cardholder data

Requirement 2: Do not use vendor-supplied defaults for system passwords and other security parameters

Protect Cardholder Data

Requirement 3: Protect stored cardholder data

Requirement 4: Encrypt transmission of cardholder data across open, public networks

Maintain a Vulnerability Management Program

Requirement 5: Use and regularly update anti-virus software

Requirement 6: Develop and maintain secure systems and applications

Implement Strong Access Control Measures

Requirement 7: Restrict access to cardholder data by business need-to-know

Requirement 8: Assign a unique ID to each person with computer access

Requirement 9: Restrict physical access to cardholder data

Regularly Monitor and Test Networks

Requirement 10: Track and monitor all access to network resources and cardholder data

Requirement 11: Regularly test security systems and processes

Maintain an Information Security Policy

Requirement 12: Maintain a policy that addresses information security

3. **Review** the following **Lab #3 Case Study on PCI DSS Non-Compliance: CardSystems Solutions**:

External hackers managed to breach a credit card transaction processing firm, resulting in the theft of privacy information. You can find information on this case against the company, CardSystems Solutions, by visiting the Federal Trade Commission's website at http://www.ftc.gov/opa/2006/02/cardsystems_r.shtm. You can find information about the PCI DSS standard and PCI DSS requirements documents by visiting https://www.pcisecuritystandards.org/security_standards/pci_dss_supporting_docs.shtml.

Case Study: CardSystems Solutions

CardSystems Solutions, a third-party payment processor, collected thousands of transactions of small and medium businesses. These transactions were then processed as batches and sent to credit card providers (such as Visa and MasterCard). The company's collection and processing of private information and financial data made it a prime target of potential hackers. Because of this, the company had to meet the data security standards that the federal, state, and industry standards require. Compliance is not optional for companies like CardSystems Solutions.

In June 2004, an external auditor certified the company as Payment Card Industry Data Security Standard (PCI DSS)-compliant. The PCI DSS standards include installing a firewall and anti-virus software and updating virus definitions on a consistent schedule. Companies must also encrypt privacy data elements. The company's certification implied that it followed a high standard of security, meaning the company used encryption methods to store privacy data. However, after the breach, a security assessment was conducted. This assessment of the security measures used at the company proved that the company was not PCI DSS-compliant.

The hacker who performed the attack used a basic exploit known as an SQL injection, which allows the hacker to place a snippet of code into the application. The hacker gained access through a Web application that customers used to access their data. With the code inserted into the fields of a form, the hacker was able to send SQL commands to the backend SQL server. The hacker wrote a script that gathered credit card data from the database, put it in a compressed zip file, and sent it to the hacker through an FTP site. The impact of the attack almost caused the company to go out of business. It had to eventually be acquired by another business.

These types of SQL injection attacks can be mitigated. Quality website design, secure coding, and internal firewalls all contribute to mitigating these types of attacks. The PCI DSS standard requires these types of mitigation controls and security methods. CardSystems was supposedly in compliance with the PCI DSS standard; however, if the company were in compliance, a successful SQL injection attack would mean the firewall was somehow circumvented.

CardSystems stored unencrypted data and failed to use proper security firewalls. It also failed to maintain its anti-virus definitions. As a result, the FTC found CardSystems Solutions and its predecessors negligent and in violation of the FTC Act 15, U.S.C. §§ 41-58.

Federal Trade Commission Act (15 U.S.C. §§ 41-58, as amended)

Under this Act, the Commission is empowered, among other things, to (a) prevent unfair methods of competition and unfair or deceptive acts or practices in or affecting commerce; (b) seek monetary redress and other relief for conduct injurious to consumers; (c) prescribe trade regulation rules defining with specificity acts or practices that are unfair or deceptive, and establishing requirements designed to prevent such acts or practices; (d) conduct investigations relating to the organization, business, practices, and management of entities engaged in commerce; and (e) make reports and legislative recommendations to Congress.

4. In your text document, **discuss** the PCI DSS requirements related to the **Lab #3 Case Study on PCI DSS Non-Compliance: CardSystems Solutions**. **Explain** which requirements weren't met and how these violate the Federal Trade Commission Act.
5. In your text document, **recommend** two or three mitigation remedies to prevent the same thing from happening at another organization.
6. **Submit** the **text document** to your instructor as a deliverable for this lab.

Evaluation Criteria and Rubrics

The following are the evaluation criteria and rubrics for Lab #3 that the students must perform:

1. Was the student able to relate a real-world case study on PCI DSS standard non-compliance and its implications? – **[25%]**
2. Was the student able to distinguish how PCI DSS is a standard and not a law, and how it defines requirements for information systems security controls and countermeasures? – **[25%]**
3. Was the student able to review a case study on a credit card transaction processing company's non-compliance with PCI DSS and identify the privacy data breach that occurred? – **[25%]**
4. Was the student able to recommend PCI DSS-compliant mitigation remedies to prevent the same loss from occurring again at a similar organization? – **[25%]**

LAB #3 – ASSESSMENT WORKSHEET

Case Study on PCI DSS Non-Compliance: CardSystems Solutions

Course Name and Number: ______________________________

Student Name: ______________________________

Instructor Name: ______________________________

Lab Due Date: ______________________________

Overview

Payment Card Industry Data Security Standard (PCI DSS) is a compliance standard that helps prevent private data breaches in companies. In this lab, you reviewed a real-world case study that involved a PCI DSS non-compliance scenario, and you recommended mitigation remedies to prevent the loss of private data for similar organizations.

Lab Assessment Questions & Answers

1. Did CardSystems Solutions break any federal or state laws?

____

____

____

____

2. In June 2004, an external auditor certified CardSystems Solutions as Payment Card Industry Data Security Standard (PCI DSS)-compliant. What is your assessment of the auditor's findings?

____

____

____

____

3. Can CardSystems Solutions sue the auditor for not performing his or her tasks and deliverables with accuracy? Do you recommend that CardSystems Solutions pursue this avenue?

4. Who do you think is negligent in this case study and why?

5. Do the actions of CardSystems Solutions warrant an "unfair trade practice" designation as stated by the Federal Trade Commission (FTC)?

6. What security policies do you recommend to help with monitoring, enforcing, and ensuring PCI DSS compliance?

7. What security controls and security countermeasures do you recommend for CardSystems Solutions to be in compliance with PCI DSS requirements?

8. What was the end result of the attack and security breach to CardSystems Solutions and its valuation?

9. What are the possible consequences associated with the data loss?

10. Who do you think is ultimately responsible for CardSystems Solutions' lack of PCI DSS compliance?

11. What should CardSystems Solutions have done to mitigate possible SQL injections and data breaches on its credit card transaction processing engine?

12. True or false: Although CardSystems Solutions had proper security controls and security countermeasures, it was not 100 percent PCI DSS-compliant because the company failed to properly implement ongoing monitoring and testing on its development and production systems.

Analyze and Compare GLBA and HIPAA

LAB 4

Introduction

The purpose of the Gramm-Leach-Bliley Act (GLBA) and the Health Insurance Portability and Accountability Act (HIPAA) is to make organizations responsible and accountable for protecting customer privacy data and implementing security controls to mitigate risks, threats, and vulnerabilities of that data. Both of these laws impact their industries significantly. In this lab, you will identify the similarities and differences of GLBA and HIPAA compliance laws, you will explain how the requirements of GLBA and HIPAA align with information systems security, you will identify privacy data elements for each, and you will describe security controls and countermeasures that support each.

Learning Objectives

Upon completing this lab, you will be able to:

- Identify the similarities between GLBA and HIPAA compliance laws
- Identify the differences between GLBA and HIPAA compliance laws
- Explain how GLBA and HIPAA requirements align with information systems security
- Identify privacy data elements for both GLBA and HIPAA
- Describe specific security controls and security countermeasures that support GLBA and HIPAA compliance

Deliverables

Upon completion of this lab, you are required to provide the following deliverables to your instructor:

1. GLBA and HIPAA Lab #4 text document;
2. Lab Assessment Questions & Answers for Lab #4.

Hands-On Steps

1. From your computer workstation, **create** a new text document called **GLBA and HIPAA Lab #4.**
2. **Launch** your Web browser. **Type** in the phrase **Gramm-Leach-Bliley Act.** Read about this act. **Research** the privacy and security rules for the Gramm-Leach-Bliley Act. In your text document, **write** a thorough description of the basic components of the Gramm-Leach Bliley Act. Be sure to include the following topics:
   - Who co-sponsored the act?
   - Who is protected by the act?
   - Who is restricted by the act?
   - How are financial institutions defined?
   - What does the act allow?
   - How would you define the major parts of the privacy requirements: the Financial Privacy Rule, the Safeguards Rule, and the pretexting provisions? What do each of these spell out in the act? (**Write** three paragraphs on each of these.)
3. In your Web browser, **research** the compliance law **HIPAA**. In your text document, **write** a thorough description of HIPAA. Be sure to include the following topics in your discussion:
   - Which U.S. government agency acts as the legal enforcement entity for HIPAA compliance violations?
   - Who is protected by HIPAA?
   - Who must comply with HIPAA?
   - What is the relevance of health care plans, providers, and clearinghouses?
   - How would you define the major parts of the Privacy Rule and the Security Rule? What do each of these spell out? (**Write** three paragraphs on each rule.)
4. In your text document, **discuss** what the GLBA and HIPAA **privacy rules** have in common. Then, **discuss** how the two are different. In your text document, **discuss** what the GLBA and HIPAA **security rules** have in common. Then, **discuss** how the two are different.
5. In your text document, **discuss** how GLBA and HIPAA requirements align with information systems security.
6. In you text document, **list** two privacy data elements for GLBA and **list** two privacy data elements for HIPAA that are under compliance.
7. In your text document, **list** two security controls or security countermeasures for GLBA and **list** two security controls or security countermeasures for HIPAA that support compliance.
8. **Submit** the **text document** to your instructor as a deliverable for this lab.

Evaluation Criteria and Rubrics

The following are the evaluation criteria and rubrics for Lab #4 that the students must perform:

1. Was the student able to identify the similarities between GLBA and HIPAA compliance laws? – **[20%]**
2. Was the student able to identify the differences between GLBA and HIPAA compliance laws? – **[20%]**
3. Was the student able to explain how GLBA and HIPAA requirements align with information systems security? – **[20%]**
4. Was the student able to identify privacy data elements for both GLBA and HIPAA? – **[20%]**
5. Was the student able to describe specific security controls and security countermeasures that support GLBA and HIPAA compliance? – **[20%]**

LAB #4 – ASSESSMENT WORKSHEET

Analyze and Compare GLBA and HIPAA

Course Name and Number: ______________________

Student Name: ______________________

Instructor Name: ______________________

Lab Due Date: ______________________

Overview

The purpose of GLBA and HIPAA is to make organizations responsible and accountable for protecting customer privacy data and implementing security controls to mitigate risks, threats, and vulnerabilities of that data. Both of these laws impact their industries significantly. In this lab, you identified the similarities and differences of GLBA and HIPAA compliance laws, you explained how the requirements of GLBA and HIPAA align with information systems security, you identified privacy data elements for each, and you described security controls and countermeasures that support each.

Lab Assessment Questions & Answers

1. Which U.S. government agency acts as the legal enforcement entity for businesses and organizations involved in commerce?

____

____

____

____

2. Which U.S. government agency acts as the legal enforcement entity regarding HIPAA compliance and HIPAA violations?

____

____

____

____

3. List three (3) similarities between GLBA and HIPAA.

4. List five (5) examples of privacy data elements for GLBA as defined in the Financial Privacy Rule.

5. List five (5) examples of privacy data elements for HIPAA as defined in the Privacy Rule.

6. List three (3) differences between GLBA and HIPAA.

7. How does GLBA's and HIPAA's privacy rule translate into information systems security controls and countermeasures?

8. What three areas does the GLBA Safeguards Rule encompass?

9. What is ePHI?

10. What three areas does the HIPAA Security Rule encompass for PHI?

11. Are organizations under GLBA and HIPAA required to mail and inform their customers in writing about their privacy rights?

12. When you go to your doctor's office, one of the forms the office asks you to fill in and sign is a HIPAA Release Form authorizing your doctor to share your medical records and privacy data with other third parties, including health insurance companies. Is this an example of the HIPAA Privacy Rule or the HIPAA Security Rule?

13. Why is a Business Associate Agreement/Contract required between a HIPAA covered entity and a downstream medical or service provider to that covered entity?

14. Like HIPAA, GLBA has both privacy and security rules. What is the official name of these rules in GLBA law?

15. True or false: GLBA encompasses insurance companies and stock brokerage firms.

Case Study on Issues Related to Sharing Consumers' Confidential Information

LAB 5

Introduction

The purpose of the Electronic Frontier Foundation (EFF) is to defend free speech, privacy, innovation, and consumer rights. In this lab you will explain the privacy issues related to an EFF case study, identify U.S. privacy law violations and their implications, and assess the impact of those violations on consumer confidential information.

Learning Objectives

Upon completing this lab, you will be able to:

- Explain the mission statement of the Electronic Frontier Foundation (EFF)
- Relate privacy issues in the case study to any personal or individual laws in the United States
- Identify U.S. citizen privacy law violations and their implications for privacy and confidential information in the case study
- Assess the impact of these violations on consumers' confidential information from a legal, ethical, and information systems security perspective

Deliverables

Upon completion of this lab, you are required to provide the following deliverables to your instructor:

1. Confidential Information Lab #5 text document;
2. Lab Assessment Questions & Answers for Lab #5.

Hands-On Steps

1. From your computer workstation, **create** a new text document called **Confidential Information Lab #5**.
2. **Review** the following **Lab #5 Case Study on Issues Related to Sharing Consumers' Confidential Information** (note that this information originated from the following Electronic Frontier Foundation Web pages: https://www.eff.org/about, https://www.eff.org/cases/hepting, and https://www.eff.org/nsa/hepting):

   From the Internet to the iPod, technologies transform society and empower us as speakers, citizens, creators, and consumers. When freedoms in the networked world come under attack, the Electronic Frontier Foundation (EFF) is the first line of defense. EFF broke new ground when it was founded in 1990—well before the Internet was on most people's radar—and continues to confront cutting-edge issues defending free speech, privacy, innovation, and consumer rights today. From the beginning, EFF has championed the public interest in every critical battle affecting digital rights.

   Blending the expertise of lawyers, policy analysts, activists, and technologists, EFF achieves significant victories on behalf of consumers and the general public. EFF fights for freedom primarily in the courts, bringing and defending lawsuits even when that means taking on the U.S. government or large corporations. By mobilizing more than 61,000 concerned citizens through the Action Center, EFF beats back bad legislation. In addition to advising policymakers, EFF educates the press and public.

   EFF is a donor-funded nonprofit and depends on support to continue successfully defending digital rights. Litigation is particularly expensive. Because two-thirds of EFF's budget comes from individual donors, every contribution is critical to helping EFF fight—and win—more cases (https://www.eff.org/about).

   EFF Case Study Information

   The Electronic Frontier Foundation (EFF) filed a class-action lawsuit against AT&T on January 31, 2006, accusing the telecom giant of violating the law and the privacy of its customers by collaborating with the National Security Agency (NSA) in its massive, illegal program to wiretap and data-mine Americans' communications. In May 2006, many other cases were filed against a variety of telecommunications companies. Subsequently the Multi-District Litigation Panel of the federal courts transferred approximately 40 cases to the Northern District of California federal court.

   In Hepting v. AT&T, EFF sued the telecommunications giant on behalf of its customers for violating privacy law by collaborating with the NSA in the massive, illegal program to wiretap and data-mine Americans' communications. Evidence in the case includes undisputed evidence provided by former AT&T telecommunications technician Mark Klein showing AT&T routed copies of Internet traffic to a secret room in San Francisco controlled by the NSA.

   In June of 2009, a federal judge dismissed Hepting and dozens of other lawsuits against telecoms, ruling that the companies had immunity from liability under the controversial FISA Amendments Act (FISAAA), which was enacted in response to court victories in Hepting. Signed by President Bush in 2008, the FISAAA allows the Attorney General to require the dismissal of the lawsuits over the telecoms' participation in the warrantless surveillance program if the government secretly certifies to the court that the surveillance did not occur, was legal, or was authorized by the president, certification that was filed in September of 2008.

   EFF plans to appeal the decision to the 9th U.S. Circuit Court of Appeals, primarily arguing that FISAAA is unconstitutional in granting to the president broad discretion to block the courts from considering the core constitutional privacy claims of millions of Americans (http://www.eff.org/cases/hepting; https://www.eff.org/nsa/hepting).

3. In your text document, **discuss** the mission statement of the Electronic Frontier Foundation (EFF).
4. In your text document, **explain** the privacy issues in the case study.
5. In your text document, **identify** the U.S. citizen privacy law violations in the case study and the implications those violations have on privacy and confidential information.
6. **Submit** the **text document** to your instructor as a deliverable for this lab.

Evaluation Criteria and Rubrics

The following are the evaluation criteria and rubrics for Lab #5 that the students must perform:

1. Was the student able to explain the mission statement of the Electronic Frontier Foundation (EFF)? – **[25%]**
2. Was the student able to relate privacy issues in the case study to any personal or individual laws in the United States? – **[25%]**
3. Was the student able to identify U.S. citizen privacy law violations and their implications for privacy and confidential information in the case study? – **[25%]**
4. Was the student able to assess the impact of these violations on consumers' confidential information from a legal, ethical, and information systems security perspective? – **[25%]**

LAB #5 – ASSESSMENT WORKSHEET

Case Study on Issues Related to Sharing Consumers' Confidential Information

Course Name and Number: ______________________________

Student Name: ______________________________

Instructor Name: ______________________________

Lab Due Date: ______________________________

Overview

The purpose of the Electronic Frontier Foundation (EFF) is to defend free speech, privacy, innovation, and consumer rights. In this lab you explained the privacy issues related to an EFF case study, identified U.S. privacy law violations and their implications, and assessed the impact of those violations on consumer confidential information.

Lab Assessment Questions & Answers

1. What is the mission statement of the Electronic Frontier Foundation?

____
____
____
____
____
____
____

2. Did the U.S. government violate the constitutional rights of U.S. citizens by ordering the NSA to review consumer confidential privacy information?

____
____
____
____

3. Why is the Hepting v. AT&T case crucial to the long-term posture of how the U.S. government can or cannot review consumer confidential information?

4. If Hepting v. AT&T results in "Big Brother" being allowed to eavesdrop and/or review the local and toll telephone dialing and bills of individuals, will U.S. citizens and consumers have any privacy rights left regarding use of communication technologies?

5. What are the legal implications of consumer privacy information being shared?

6. What are the ethical implications of consumer privacy information being shared?

7. What are the information systems security implications of consumer information being shared?

8. What law allowed a federal judge to dismiss Hepting vs. AT&T and other lawsuits against telecommunication service providers participating in the warrantless surveillance program authorized by the president?

9. True or false: EFF claimed that the ruling set forth by FISAAA was unconstitutional.

Identify the Scope of Your State's Data and Security Breach Notification Law

LAB 6

Introduction

The purpose of the National Conference of State Legislatures (NCSL) is, according to its website, to provide "access to current state and federal legislation and a comprehensive list of state documents, including state statutes, constitutions, legislative audits, and research reports." In this lab, you will review the data security breach notification laws for your state and you will assess the scope and depth of the privacy protection rights of a citizen in your state.

Learning Objectives

Upon completing this lab, you will be able to:

- Relate state government data security breach notification laws to individual privacy
- Explain why state governments have data security breach notification laws
- Find a specific state's data and security breach notification law
- Download a copy of a specific state's data and security breach notification law
- Assess the scope and depth of the privacy protection rights of a citizen of any particular state

Deliverables

Upon completion of this lab, you are required to provide the following deliverables to your instructor:

1. State Government Lab #6 text document;
2. Lab Assessment Questions & Answers for Lab #6.

Hands-On Steps

1. From your computer workstation, **create** a new text document called **State Government Lab #6**.
2. Currently, 46 states, the District of Columbia, Guam, Puerto Rico, and the U.S. Virgin Islands have data and security breach notification laws that define what organizations must do if they have had data or security breached that impact citizen privacy data. The National Conference of State Legislatures (NCSL) website tracks and organizes telecommunication and information technology state legislation. **Review** the NCSL website and data and security breach notification laws for each state listed at **http://www.ncsl.org/IssuesResearch/TelecommunicationsInformation Technology/SecurityBreachNotificationLaws/tabid/13489/Default.aspx**.
3. **Scroll** down the list of states and **find** the state of Virginia. **Click** the **Va. Code § 18.2-186.6 link**. **Review** the security breach notification law. In your text document, **explain** how state government data security breach notification laws relate to individual privacy.
4. **Click** the **Back button** on your browser. After you have returned to the list of states, scroll to find your state. **Click** and **download** the security breach notification laws for your state. If you cannot download your state's security breach laws, return to the state of Virginia and use that information to complete this lab.
5. In your text document, **discuss** the privacy protection rights that a citizen in your state has.
6. **Submit** the **text document** to your instructor as a deliverable for this lab.

Evaluation Criteria and Rubrics

The following are the evaluation criteria and rubrics for Lab #6 that the students must perform:

1. Was the student able to relate state government data security breach notification laws to individual privacy? – **[20%]**
2. Was the student able to explain why state governments have data security breach notification laws? – **[20%]**
3. Was the student able to find his or her state's data and security breach notification law? – **[20%]**
4. Was the student able to download a copy of his or her state's data and security breach notification law? – **[20%]**
5. Was the student able to assess the scope and depth of the privacy protection rights of a citizen of any particular state? – **[20%]**

LAB #6 – ASSESSMENT WORKSHEET

Identify the Scope of Your State's Data and Security Breach Notification Law

Course Name and Number: ______________________________

Student Name: ______________________________

Instructor Name: ______________________________

Lab Due Date: ______________________________

Overview

The purpose of the National Conference of State Legislatures (NCSL) is, according to its website, to provide "access to current state and federal legislation and a comprehensive list of state documents, including state statutes, constitutions, legislative audits, and research reports." In this lab, you reviewed the data security breach notification laws for your state and you assessed the scope and depth of the privacy protection rights of a citizen in your state.

Lab Assessment Questions & Answers

1. Were you successful in finding your state's data and security breach notification law? Specify the name of the law and the date of its ratification. If you were unable to download your state's law, use the state of Virginia to complete the question.

____

____

____

____

2. What is the purpose of state governments imposing a breach notification law on organizations to protect its citizens?

____

____

____

____

____

3. Explain how state government data security breach notification laws relate to individual privacy.

4. Assess the scope and depth of privacy protection rights that a citizen has by being a resident of a state. Write down the name of your state, and then identify the following for your state's breach notification law:

- Who or what does the law in your state protect?

- Does the law include both for profit and nonprofit organizations?

- Does the law have a financial penalty assessed to the negligent party if proven guilty?

- Does your state require the organization to publicly announce a breach to the media?

- Does your state notification law take into account encrypted data or doesn't it matter whether the data is encrypted or not encrypted?

- Does your state's law define the amount of time an organization has to publicly announce that a breach has occurred? If yes, specify the time. If no, describe how your state handles this.

5. True or false: If you are a citizen in one state but the company that had a data and security breach with your privacy data resides in another, the company must adhere to the data and security breach notification law of your home state.

6. Because most states have data and security breach notification laws related to their citizens' privacy, what is the number one reason for having these laws from a citizen protection perspective?

7. Some states define a data and security breach as the loss and exposure of citizen privacy data in an unencrypted manner. If a state encountered a data and security breach, but no citizen privacy data was compromised given that it was encrypted in a steady-state within a database, does the company or organization have to abide by the data and security breach notification law?

8. True or false: Unauthorized access to a system must occur for the data and security breach notification law to take precedence.

Case Study on Digital Millennium Copyright Act: Napster

LAB 7

Introduction

The purpose of the Digital Millennium Copyright Act is to implement treaties signed at the World Intellectual Property Organization Geneva conference. It has several provisions meant to protect copyrighted works and access to them. In this lab, you will review the Digital Millennium Copyright Act and its provisions. You will also review a case study involving Napster, a company that violated the Digital Millennium Copyright Act.

Learning Objectives

Upon completing this lab, you will be able to:

- Describe the highlights of the Digital Millennium Copyright Act and its provisions
- Relate the Digital Millennium Copyright Act to the Napster music piracy case
- Explain why Napster was not able to hide behind the defense of the Digital Millennium Copyright Act
- Assess the impact of violations of copyright and the Digital Millennium Copyright Act from a legal, ethical, and information systems security perspective

Deliverables

Upon completion of this lab, you are required to provide the following deliverables to your instructor:

1. Napster Lab #7 text document;
2. Lab Assessment Questions & Answers for Lab #7.

Hands-On Steps

1. From your computer workstation, **create** a new text document called **Napster Lab #7**.
2. **Review** the following **Lab#7 Case Study on the Digital Millennium Copyright Act: Napster:**

   Napster was a company that used peer-to-peer networking to provide a file-sharing service that gave its users the ability to share music. The company existed only from June 1999 to July 2001.

   In December 1999, the Recording Industry Association of America (RIAA) took legal action against Napster for copyright infringements. RIAA, the plaintiff, represented all major record labels in this action. It claimed that Napster violated "exclusive rights for reproduction and distribution of their copyright works." RIAA claimed that Napster made a "direct" infringement on its copyright and that it was liable for "contributory infringement of the plaintiff's copyright" and for "vicarious infringement of the plaintiff's copyright."

   The law that stopped Napster from continuing its operations is the Digital Millennium Copyright Act that was enacted in 1998. The Act addresses treaties signed in 1996 at the World Intellectual Property Organization (WIPO) Geneva conference and it contains other provisions. Software and entertainment industries supported the law, but many others opposed it, including academics, scientists, and librarians. Following are key components of the act:

   - It is a crime to circumvent anti-piracy measures in commercial software
   - The manufacture, sale, or distribution of code-cracking devices used to illegally copy software is illegal
   - Copyright protection devices may be cracked for the purposes of encryption research, to assess product interoperability, and for the purposes of testing security systems
   - Under certain conditions, anti-circumvention provisions exempt nonprofit libraries, archives, and educational institutions
   - Internet service providers are protected from copyright infringement liability for the act of transmitting information over the Internet
   - Website content that appears to infringe copyright law can be removed
   - Nonprofit institutions of higher education are protected from liability when faculty and students infringe on copyright
   - "Webcasters" must pay licensing fees to record companies
   - The Register of Copyrights, upon consulting with relevant parties, must provide Congress recommendations for "how to promote distance education through digital technologies" while "maintaining an appropriate balance between the rights of copyright owners and the needs of users"
   - It says that "nothing in this section shall affect rights, remedies, limitations, or defenses to copyright infringement, including fair use"
3. **Launch** your Web browser. **Research** the Napster case. In your text document, discuss the case and be sure to include the following topics:
   - How did Napster try to defend itself against RIAA's claims?
   - What does contributory infringement of copyright mean and how did this affect Napster?
   - What does material contribution mean and how did this affect Napster?
   - What was the court's decision about the case? What became of Napster?
4. In your text document, **discuss** the provisions of the Digital Millennium Copyright Act. In your text document, **explain** how the Digital Millennium Copyright Act affected the Napster music piracy case.
5. In your text document, **discuss** the impact you think this case study has from a legal, ethical, and information systems security perspective.
6. **Submit** the **text document** to your instructor as a deliverable for this lab.

Evaluation Criteria and Rubrics

The following are the evaluation criteria and rubrics for Lab #7 that the students must perform:

1. Was the student able to describe the highlights of the Digital Millennium Copyright Act and its provisions? – **[25%]**
2. Was the student able to relate the Digital Millennium Copyright Act to the Napster music piracy case? – **[25%]**
3. Was the student able to explain why Napster was not able to hide behind the defense of the Digital Millennium Copyright Act? – **[25%]**
4. Was the student able to assess the impact of violations of copyright and the Digital Millennium Copyright Act from a legal, ethical, and information systems security perspective? – **[25%]**

LAB #7 – ASSESSMENT WORKSHEET

Case Study on Digital Millennium Copyright Act: Napster

Course Name and Number: ______________________________

Student Name: ______________________________

Instructor Name: ______________________________

Lab Due Date: ______________________________

Overview

The purpose of the Digital Millennium Copyright Act is to implement treaties signed at the World Intellectual Property Organization Geneva conference. It has several provisions meant to protect copyrighted works and access to them. In this lab, you reviewed the Digital Millennium Copyright Act and its provisions. You also reviewed a case study involving Napster, a company that violated the Digital Millennium Copyright Act.

Lab Assessment Questions & Answers

1. What was the premise behind the Recording Industry Association of America's lawsuit against Napster?

____

____

____

____

2. Based on your knowledge of how Napster works, if you downloaded a copy of a song from a friend's hard drive using Napster, would you be infringing on the musician's or record company's copyright?

____

____

____

____

3. Describe the scope of the Digital Millennium Copyright Act and what or whom it protects.

4. What was the link between the Digital Millennium Copyright Act and the Napster legal proceedings?

5. What are the legal implications of Napster's online music-sharing service?

6. What are the ethical implications of Napster's online music-sharing service?

7. What are the information systems security implications of Napster's service?

8. Why did Napster ultimately have to shut down its services?

9. True or false: Napster obtained direct financial benefit from the infringement of users.

10. If Napster acted as a distributor and provided backend royalties through the RIAA to the original owners of copyrights to the music, do you think Napster would still be in existence and possibly one of the largest online music distributors?

LAB 8

Cyberstalking or Cyberbullying and Laws to Protect Individuals

Introduction

Cyberstalking and cyberbullying are not just terms for today's youth. They are real and increasing threats online. This is particularly true with social media, social communications, and social networking being done online. Protecting your identity, your privacy, and your data is a requirement for interacting and socializing online. In this lab, you will define cyberstalking and cyberbullying and describe their legal implications, you will identify case studies for cyberstalking and cyberbullying, and you will define the requirements for a law to protect individuals from both of these threats.

Learning Objectives

Upon completing this lab, you will be able to:

- Define cyberstalking and describe the legal implications of cyberstalking an individual
- Define cyberbullying and describe the legal implications of cyberbullying an individual
- Identify case studies on cyberstalking and cyberbullying on the Internet
- Define the requirements for a law to protect individuals from cyberstalking or cyberbullying

Deliverables

Upon completion of this lab, you are required to provide the following deliverables to your instructor:

1. Cyberstalking Lab #8 text document;
2. Lab Assessment Questions & Answers for Lab #8.

Hands-On Steps

1. From your computer workstation, **create** a new text document called **Cyberstalking Lab #8**.
2. **Launch** your Web browser. Then, **search** the term **cyberstalking.** In your text document, **define** what **cyberstalking** means. In your text document, **discuss** the legal implications of cyberstalking.
3. After you have defined the term cyberstalking, **search** the Internet for a **cyberstalking** case. In your text document, **discuss** this case. **Explain** the case, who was victimized, and how the person was victimized. Then, **discuss** how you would protect this individual from the scenario presented in the case by outlining the law you would create.
4. **Search** the term **cyberbullying.** In your text document, **define** what **cyberbullying** means. In your text document, **discuss** the legal implications of cyberbullying.
5. After you have defined the term **cyberbullying**, **search** the Internet for a **cyberbullying** case. In your text document, **discuss** this case. **Explain** the case, who was victimized, and how the person was victimized. Then, **discuss** how you would protect this individual from the scenario presented in the case by outlining the law you would create.
6. **Submit** the **text document** to your instructor as a deliverable for this lab.

Evaluation Criteria and Rubrics

The following are the evaluation criteria and rubrics for Lab #8 that the students must perform:

1. Was the student able to define cyberstalking and describe the legal implications of cyberstalking an individual? – **[25%]**
2. Was the student able to define cyberbullying and describe the legal implications of cyberbullying an individual? – **[25%]**
3. Was the student able to identify case studies on cyberstalking and cyberbullying on the Internet? – **[25%]**
4. Was the student able to define the requirements for a law to protect individuals from cyberstalking or cyberbullying? – **[25%]**

LAB #8 – ASSESSMENT WORKSHEET

Cyberstalking or Cyberbullying and Laws to Protect Individuals

Course Name and Number: ______________________________

Student Name: ______________________________

Instructor Name: ______________________________

Lab Due Date: ______________________________

Overview

Cyberstalking and cyberbullying are not just terms for today's youth. They are real and increasing threats online. This is particularly true with social media, social communications, and social networking being done online. Protecting your identity, your privacy, and your data is a requirement for interacting and socializing online. In this lab, you defined cyberstalking and cyberbullying and described their legal implications, you identified case studies for cyberstalking and cyberbullying, and you defined the requirements for a law to protect individuals from both of these threats.

Lab Assessment Questions & Answers

1. Define cyberstalking.

____

____

____

____

____

2. Define cyberbullying.

____

____

____

____

____

3. List the name of one of your case studies. Download a copy of it and insert the case study here.

4. Summarize your case study in one paragraph, highlighting the cyberstalking or cyberbullying scenario.

5. If you were to draft a law, what elements of that law would you include to protect individuals from the actions and outcomes occurring in your particular case?

Recommend IT Security Policies to Help Mitigate Risk

LAB 9

Introduction

The purpose of security policies is to help mitigate the identified risks. Writing these policies is easier once you have created an asset inventory list, prioritized that list, and identified the major risk exposures found in those assets. In this lab, you will create a high-level IT asset inventory list, prioritize those assets, identify the risk exposures, and make recommendations for policies that can mitigate the risk exposures.

Learning Objectives

Upon completing this lab, you will be able to:

- Create a high-level IT asset inventory list
- Prioritize the IT assets in terms of importance to a school's operation and business
- Identify the top five (5) risk exposures found in the high-level IT asset assessment
- Recommend IT security policies that can help mitigate the identified risk exposures

Deliverables

Upon completion of this lab, you are required to provide the following deliverables to your instructor:

1. Security Policies Lab #9 text document;
2. Lab Assessment Questions & Answers for Lab #9.

Hands-On Steps

1. From your computer workstation, **create** a new text document called **Security Policies Lab #9**.
2. **Review** the following scenario for Premier Collegiate School. In your text document, **list** the risk elements at the school.

   Case Study: Premier Collegiate School

   You are the new Director for Information Technology at Premier Collegiate School. The private school teaches grade 7 to grade 12 with 300 students and 30 staff members and faculty. Each of the 10 administrative staff members has a dedicated desktop computer. The school's principal has a notebook computer that she takes home and when traveling to conduct both school business and personal tasks. She maintains a Facebook™ account and has opened a MySpace™ account to monitor the activities of the students who also have such accounts. The teachers have 10 computers that they share in the teacher's lounge to record grades and do all work associated with conducting their assigned classes (daily lesson plans, research, handouts, tests, quizzes, and final exams).

   The school has two file servers. One is for administration business and the other serves student computing needs. The administration server has dedicated storage for each of the teachers and both hardwired access and wireless LAN access throughout the school. The student server has applications the students might need for their school work, and provides wireless access for student-owned laptop computers. All students are required to have a laptop computer with wireless access. In addition, the school has a dedicated computer lab with 25 desktop computers for the students to use in computer science classes.
3. The school's principal has requested that you prepare an IT asset list and a high-level prioritization or ranking of the IT assets given the function and purpose for administrative or student computing requirements. Based on your experience and knowledge of schools, **prepare** a comprehensive **asset list**. Then, **determine** the importance of each asset to the school function by **ranking** its placement on the list (starting with 1 as the most important, 2 as the second most important, and so on).

   Keep in mind that assets include more than just physical objects you can hold. Do not forget that assets include electronic information, such as student records, lesson plans, test banks, and so on. Assets also include key personnel, such as knowledgeable instructors and important administrators.

Using the figure (Figure 9.1) that follows the table below, **identify** which of the **seven domains** of a typical IT infrastructure each asset resides in. The data, systems, or applications may have student privacy data elements. In the table, **perform** a high-level **FERPA compliance assessment** (FERPA is the Family Educational Rights and Privacy Act) identifying where student privacy data resides and assessing the security controls protecting that data. Finally, **prioritize** the asset by assigning it a **critical, major, or minor** classification.

IT ASSET DESCRIPTION	RANKING OF IT ASSET	ONE OF SEVEN DOMAINS	FERPA PRIVACY DATA IMPACT	ASSESSMENT [CRITICAL-MAJOR-MINOR]

FIGURE 9.1
Seven domains of a typical IT infrastructure

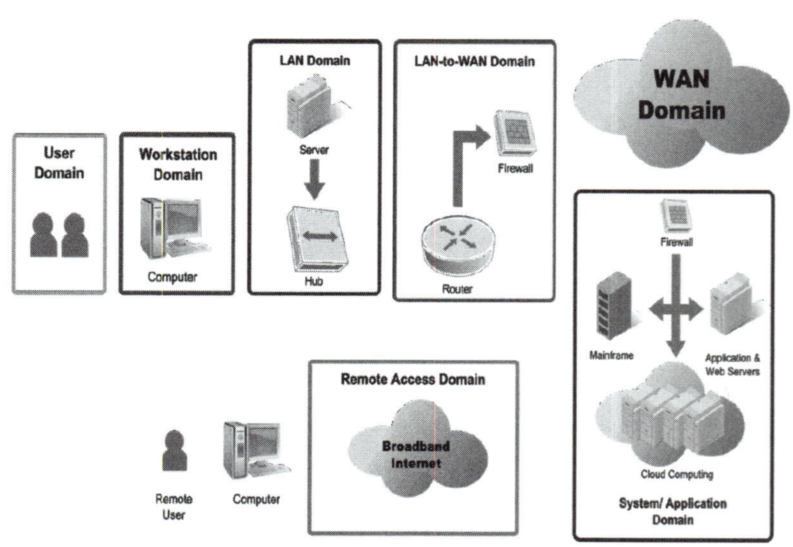

4. In your text document, **list** three recommendations for **IT security policies** to help mitigate the risk exposures in the school's IT infrastructure.
5. **Submit** the **text document** to your instructor as a deliverable for this lab.

Evaluation Criteria and Rubrics

The following are the evaluation criteria and rubrics for Lab #9 that the students must perform:

1. Was the student able to create a high-level IT asset inventory list? – [**25%**]
2. Was the student able to prioritize the IT assets in terms of importance to a school's operation and business? – [**25%**]
3. Was the student able to identify the top five (5) risk exposures found in the high-level IT asset assessment? – [**25%**]
4. Was the student able to recommend IT security policies that can help mitigate the identified risk exposures? – [**25%**]

LAB #9 – ASSESSMENT WORKSHEET

Recommend IT Security Policies to Help Mitigate Risk

Course Name and Number: _______________

Student Name: _______________

Instructor Name: _______________

Lab Due Date: _______________

Overview

The purpose of security policies is to help mitigate the identified risks. Writing these policies is easier once you have created an asset inventory list, prioritized that list, and identified the major risk exposures found in those assets. In this lab, you created a high-level IT asset inventory list, prioritized those assets, identified the risk exposures, and made recommendations for policies that can mitigate the risk exposures.

Lab Assessment Questions & Answers

1. Which IT assets did you prioritize as critical to administrative or student computing?

2. List your top five (5) risk exposures for which you believe this school should have specific risk-mitigation strategies.

3. Given the potential risks that you identified, what IT security policies would you recommend that the school create to help mitigate each of the identified risk exposures you listed in question #2?

4. True or false: FERPA compliance law is about protecting the privacy data of students, including personal information, grades, and transcripts. The law itself defines a privacy requirement but it does not specifically address security controls and security countermeasures.

5. Given that student privacy data is typically housed within administrative computers, systems, and databases, what can you do to mitigate the risk exposure that a student or someone on the student or school's network can access these systems?

6. For a school under FERPA compliance law, do you think the administrative computing or student computing network infrastructure is more important from a business and delivery of education perspective?

7. The school monitors the use of student social networking on Facebook, MySpace, and Twitter. What should the school define and implement if it wants to define acceptable and unacceptable use of school IT assets, Internet, e-mail, and use of personal laptop computers on the school's network?

___

___

___

___

Case Study in Computer Forensics: Pharmaceutical Company

LAB 10

Introduction

The purpose of chain of custody procedures is to protect evidence that might be used in a court of law. In this lab, you will look at the chain of custody procedures for digital evidence, review a computer forensics case study, and create a security incident response form to capture the steps needed to maintain chain of custody.

Learning Objectives

Upon completing this lab, you will be able to:

- Identify the key steps in maintaining chain of custody for digital evidence used in a court of law
- Review a computer forensics case study and identify how and what evidence was captured
- Relate chain of custody to a computer forensics case study for using digital evidence in a court of law
- Create a security incident response form capturing the steps needed to maintain chain of custody integrity when responding to a security breach

Deliverables

Upon completion of this lab, you are required to provide the following deliverables to your instructor:

1. Chain of Custody Lab #10 text document;
2. Lab Assessment Questions & Answers for Lab #10.

Hands-On Steps

1. From your computer workstation, **create** a new text document called **Chain of Custody Lab #10**.
2. **Review** the following **Lab #10 Case Study in Computer Forensics: Pharmaceutical Company** (the text for this case study originated at http://www.evestigate.com/Case_Studies/Case%20Study%20Prescription%20Drug%20Diversion%20Brand%20Protection.pdf; this case study can be freely distributed if no portion of it has been changed, including the following contact information: Toll Free: 1-800-868-8189; Int. Phone: Phone 727-287-6000; http://www.evestigate.com):

   (Global Digital Forensics—GDF—is a computer forensics consulting firm that is referenced throughout the case study below.)

   Global Digital Forensics Case Study Drug Diversion

   Case Type: Prescription Drug Diversion, Anti-Counterfeit, Brand Protection, and International Computer Forensics

   Environment: On-Site Seizure at Several Locations throughout the United States and Canada

   Industry: Pharmaceutical

   Systems Involved: Desktops, Laptops, E-mail, Handheld Devices, and E-mail

   Case Background

   A pharmaceutical company began receiving complaints from its representatives in certain geographical areas that sales of normally high-volume drugs were slowing down considerably. The company's internal security department as well as the security departments of its major distributors began an investigation. The results of the investigation led the security professionals to believe a significant amount of the company's products were being diverted from foreign countries into the United States and sold through smaller distributors who specialized in sales to locally, privately owned pharmacies and dispensaries in nursing homes. The diversion activities were immediately reported to the local authorities in the regions as well as to the FDA.

   An investigation was immediately launched and millions of dollars of diverted drugs and repackaging equipment was seized from several locations, including the warehouses of fully licensed pharmaceutical distributors. Along with the diverted product, the computers and other electronic equipment were also seized.

   The seizure went smoothly and the company was satisfied as were investigators from the FDA and local law enforcement. However, the case was severely hindered by the fact that the majority of communications between the principals of the distribution companies (foreign nationals) and the foreign suppliers was conducted by e-mail. There were also no significant paper records on site. While the local authorities and the FDA had access to computer forensic labs, both faced similar roadblocks in their investigations. The labs were severely backlogged and the systems were encrypted, fairly complex, and recorded in a foreign language.

   It became obvious that the investigation would be delayed until one of the labs cleared some high-priority cases and could dedicate the time required to forensically analyze the computers from the seizure. Time was of the essence. Everyone knew that the computer forensics had to begin immediately if the diversion was to cease and the case successfully prosecuted. Because the suspects claimed they were reshipping the drugs outside the U.S. (a legal practice) and had shipping bills that appeared to back this statement up, documentation from the computers was essential. If computer forensic analysis was delayed, it was almost assured that the U.S. Attorney's Office would drop the charges.

GDF Involvement

The company called in GDF and, working in cooperation with the local authorities as well as with the FDA and U.S. Attorney's Office, GDF was able to commence computer forensic analysis of the computers seized at the pharmaceutical warehouses and provide the information and artifacts recovered during the computer forensic analysis to the U.S. Attorney's Office.

GDF dispatched a Mobile Computer Forensics Lab and, along with investigators from the U.S Attorney's Office, created forensically sound copies of the hard drives seized from the warehouses to be used to conduct the computer forensic analysis. Strict chain of custody was maintained and the computer forensics was conducted under the supervision of the U.S. Attorney's Office following all accepted computer forensic methodologies.

The Findings

GDF Computer Forensic Specialists were able to decrypt and extract a wealth of information from the systems that were forensically analyzed. By conducting a complete computer forensic analysis of all the data the hard disks contained, GDF was able to provide documentation showing that the diverted drugs were being purchased from distributors in Europe and Canada and being shipped to the U.S. in what appeared to be legitimate transactions. The computer forensic analysis also showed that the distributor had purchased equipment to unwrap the foreign drugs as well as repackaging equipment, all signs of a legitimate drug repackaging and exporting company.

GDF's computer forensic analysts were also able to extract documents showing that the owners of the distributors also controlled several pharmacies in the area as well as several nursing homes and ACLF facilities, all of which appeared to purchase drugs from the distributors. There were also many invoices for custom vitamins shipped to another distributor just two buildings away that appeared to be controlled by the suspects.

The Outcome

Using the digital evidence the computer forensic specialists gathered, along with the physical evidence, the United States Attorney was able to prove:

1. The distributor was purchasing drugs from foreign sources to be sold within the United States
2. The distributors were engaged in drug diversion for over 10 years
3. The distributor was repackaging vitamins manufactured to appear the same as the prescription drugs and selling and shipping them to Asia
4. The distributor was operating unlicensed pharmacies and nursing homes

The primary pharmaceutical company sustained over 13 million dollars a year in lost revenue. In addition, the suspects distributed millions of dollars in counterfeit drugs throughout Asia, potentially endangering the lives of hundreds of innocent people.

The suspects were convicted and sentenced in the United States and being investigated in five (5) other countries.

3. **Launch** your Web browser. **Search** for the phrase **"Chain of Custody for Digital Evidence."** In your text document, **define** the phrase chain of custody. Next, **paraphrase** what you found for your search of **"Chain of Custody for Digital Evidence."**

4. In your browser, **search** for **"Security Incident Response Forms"** to find examples of how and what data needs to be captured from one step or task to the next to follow the proper chain of custody that includes sequencing and time/date stamp logging. In your text document and using the following table, **create** a **Security Incident Response Form** that captures the chain of custody procedures for the workstations, laptops, e-mail, and handheld devices for each individual in the case study. To follow chain of custody procedures, in the form, **address** the **individual identity or user of the equipment, model, make, serial #, operating systems, applications, and so on**. To follow chain of custody procedures, the form should also answer the following questions (each of these should be accompanied with a date and timestamp):
   - What is the evidence?
   - How did you get it?
   - When was it collected?
   - Who has handled it?
   - Why did that person handle it?
   - Where has it traveled, and where was it ultimately stored?

SECURITY INCIDENT RESPONSE FORENSICS CHECKLIST

> **Note:**
> This form or checklist can be used for workstations and servers and other IT assets (for example, switches, routers, firewalls, other assets) that have been affected by a security incident or breach.

Example "Activities" are listed in the template.

INITIALS	DATE	TIME	ACTIVITY
			Wipe, Partition, and Format TARGET Media
Serial Number:			
Software:			
Partition Notes:			
INITIALS	**DATE**	**TIME**	**ACTIVITY**
			Create Forensic Boot Disk
Notes:			

(*Continues*)

(Continued)

INITIALS	DATE	TIME	ACTIVITY
			Verify Software License
License Information:			
Notes:			

INITIALS	DATE	TIME	ACTIVITY
			Physical Examination of SOURCE Computer
Location:			
Make & Model:			
Serial #:			
Condition (On/Off, Damage):			
Owner/User:			
Notes:			

INITIALS	DATE	TIME	ACTIVITY
			Source CMOS Examined
Clock:			
Notes:			

INITIALS	DATE	TIME	ACTIVITY
			Hard Disk(s) Removed (Unplugged/ Prevents Booting from Source)
Notes:			

(Continues)

(Continued)

INITIALS	DATE	TIME	ACTIVITY
			Hard Disk Information (how many?)
Number of Drives:			
Make:			
Capacity:			
Serial #:			
Bagged (Antistatic/Evidence Tape):			
Name of Custodian:			
Storage Location:			
Notes:			

INITIALS	DATE	TIME	ACTIVITY
			Description of Collection System From/To Imaging
Notes:			

INITIALS	DATE	TIME	ACTIVITY
			Image Made
Software:			
Details of Evidence Report:			
Number of Images:			
Notes:			

(*Continues*)

(Continued)

INITIALS	DATE	TIME	ACTIVITY
			File Listing
Notes:			

INITIALS	DATE	TIME	ACTIVITY
			Deleted File Recovery
Notes:			

5. **Submit** the **text document** to your instructor as a deliverable for this lab.

Evaluation Criteria and Rubrics

The following are the evaluation criteria and rubrics for Lab #10 that the students must perform:

1. Was the student able to identify the key steps in maintaining chain of custody for digital evidence used in a court of law? – [**25%**]
2. Was the student able to review a computer forensics case study and identify how and what evidence was captured? – [**25%**]
3. Was the student able to relate chain of custody to a computer forensics case study for using digital evidence in a court of law? – [**25%**]
4. Was the student able to create a security incident response form capturing the steps needed to maintain chain of custody integrity when responding to a security breach? – [**25%**]

LAB #10 – ASSESSMENT WORKSHEET

Case Study in Computer Forensics: Pharmaceutical Company

Course Name and Number: ______________________________

Student Name: ______________________________

Instructor Name: ______________________________

Lab Due Date: ______________________________

Overview

The purpose of chain of custody procedures is to protect evidence that might be used in a court of law. In this lab, you looked at the chain of custody procedures for digital evidence, reviewed a computer forensics case study, and created a security incident response form to capture the steps needed to maintain chain of custody.

Lab Assessment Questions & Answers

1. List the steps in maintaining chain of custody for digital evidence.

____
____
____
____
____

2. Why is it important to follow the chain of custody when gathering evidence?

____
____
____
____
____

3. For the computer forensics case, identify what evidence the forensics experts were able to gather.

4. Name two of the things the United States Attorney was able to prove in the computer forensics case.

5. What important questions should the security incident response form answer?

6. Why is it important to include a date and timestamp in the security incident response form?